KT-456-533

I Like Cats

ROTHERHAM
PUBLIC
LIBRARY
B48
R000-74607

Angela Aylmore

Heinemann
LIBRARY

www.heinemann.co.uk/library
Visit our website to find out more information about Heinemann Library books.

To order:
☎ Phone 44 (0) 1865 888066
Send a fax to 44 (0) 1865 314091
📄 Visit the Heinemann Bookshop at www.heinemann.co.uk/library to browse our
💻 catalogue and order online.

First published in Great Britain by Heinemann Library,
Halley Court, Jordan Hill, Oxford OX2 8EJ, part
of Harcourt Education. Heinemann is a registered
trademark of Harcourt Education Ltd.

© Harcourt Education Ltd 2007
The moral right of the proprietor has been asserted.

All rights reserved. No part of this publication may be
reproduced, stored in a retrieval system, or transmitted
in any form or by any means, electronic, mechanical,
photocopying, recording, or otherwise, without either
the prior written permission of the publishers or a
licence permitting restricted copying in the United
Kingdom issued by the Copyright Licensing Agency Ltd,
90 Tottenham Court Road, London W1T 4LP
(www.cla.co.uk).

Editorial: Dan Nunn and Sarah Chappelow
Design: Joanna Hinton-Malivoire
Picture research: Erica Newbery
Production: Duncan Gilbert

Origination: Chroma Graphics (Overseas) Pte. Ltd
Printed and bound in China by South
China Printing Co. Ltd.

10-digit ISBN 0 431 10959 1
13-digit ISBN 978 0 431 10959 6
11 10 09 08 07
10 9 8 7 6 5 4 3 2 1

British Library Cataloguing in Publication Data
Aylmore, Angela
I like cats. - (Things I like)
1. Cats - Juvenile literature
I. Title
636.8
A full catalogue record for this book is available from
the British Library.

Acknowledgements
The publishers would like to thank the following for
permission to reproduce photographs: Ardea pp. **7**
(John Daniels), **9** (John Daniels), **14** (John Daniels);
Digital Vision p. **21** (spotted leopard); FLPA p. **21** (black
leopard, Jurgen & Christine Sohns); Getty Images pp.
4–5 (all, Photodisc), **10** (Brand X pictures), **11** (Dorling
Kindersley), **15** (Photodisc), **16** (The Image Bank),
22 (kitten, Photodisc); Nature Picture Library pp. **17**
(Jane Burton), **18** (Anup Shah), **20** (Lucasseck/ARCO);
NHPA pp. **19** (Andy Rouse), **22** (lion, Andy Rouse);
Photolibrary p. **6** (Dennie & DK. Cody/Workbook, Inc.);
Ron Kimball Stock pp. **8** (Ron Kimball), **22** (Himalayan
cat, Ron Kimball); Warren Photographic pp. **12–13**.

Cover photograph of a cat reproduced with permission
of Alamy/Creatas/Dynamic Graphics Group.

Every effort has been made to contact copyright holders
of any material reproduced in this book. Any omissions
will be rectified in subsequent printings if notice is given
to the publishers.

Contents

Some words are shown in bold, **like this**. You can find out what they mean by looking in the Glossary.

Cats

I like cats.

I will tell you my favourite things about cats.

Different cats

I like the way cats are so different. This Siamese cat has big green eyes.

Bobtail cats have a stubby tail.

Himalayan cats have long
fur and a cute face.

I like this cat the best.
It is a Sphynx cat. It has
no hair and big ears!

Taking care of my cat

I like taking care of my cat.
My cat likes to be **stroked**.

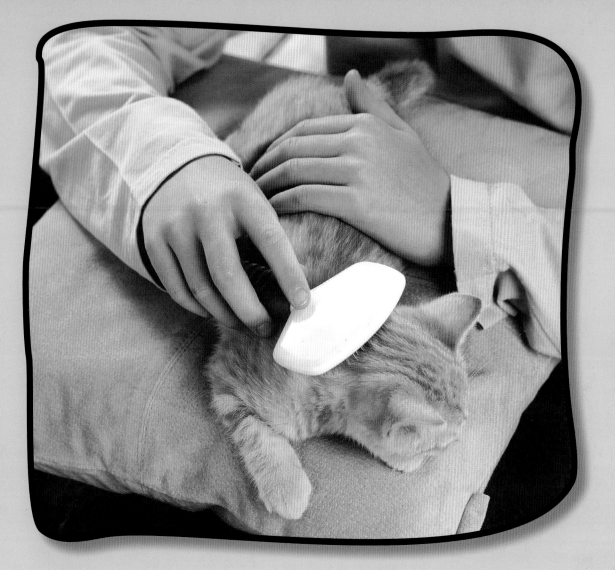

My cat has long fur. I brush the fur to keep it clean.

I feed my cat twice a day.
I make sure my cat has
water to drink.

13

Kittens

My cat has had **kittens**.
The kittens are very small!

I really like kittens. Kittens have small noses and **whiskers**.

15

Kittens look cute. But kittens have sharp **claws!**

Kittens use their claws
to play with toys.

Wild cats

A tiger is a big cat. I like tigers. Tigers hide in the grass.

I like lions too. Male lions have an enormous **mane**!

Cheetahs are very fast. Cheetahs can run as fast as a car!

These are both leopards. Some have spots and some are all black.

Do you like cats?

Now you know why I like cats! Do you like cats too?

Glossary

claw a hard, sharp nail on a cat's foot

kitten a baby cat

mane long hair on the neck of some animals, like lions and horses

stroke to move your hand over something gently

stubby short and thick

whiskers long, stiff hairs that grow on a cat's face

Find out more

Care for Your Kitten (RSPCA Pet Guides),
Heather Thomas (Collins, 2004)

Cats and Kittens, Katherine Starke
(Usborne Publishing, 2004)

Index

Titles in the *Things I Like* series include:

Hardback   978 0 4311 0960 2

Hardback   978 0 4311 0957 2

Hardback   978 0 4311 0959 6

Hardback   978 0 4311 0953 4

Hardback   978 0 4311 0958 9

Hardback   978 0 4311 0954 1

Hardback   978 0 4311 0956 5

Hardback   978 0 4311 0955 8

Find out about other titles from Heinemann Library on our website www.heinemann.co.uk/library